The Unspoken Emotions

Riya Ramudamu

Rajmangal Prakashan

An Imprint of **Rajmangal Publishers**

Price : 129/-

ISBN : 978-9394920972

Published by :

Rajmangal Publishers

Rajmangal Prakashan Building,
1st Street, Sangwan, Quarsi, Ramghat Road
Aligarh-202001, (UP) INDIA
Cont. No. +91- 7017993445
www.rajmangalpublishers.com
rajmangalpublishers@gmail.com
sampadak@rajmangalpublishers.in

प्रथम संस्करण : जनवरी 2023 – पेपरबैक

प्रकाशक : राजमंगल प्रकाशन

राजमंगल प्रकाशन बिल्डिंग, 1st स्ट्रीट,

सांगवान, क्वार्सी, रामघाट रोड,

अलीगढ़, उप्र. – 202001, भारत

फ़ोन : +91 - 7017993445

First Published : Jan. 2023 - Paperback
Printed by : Thomson Press India Ltd, Repro India Ltd & Manipal Tech Ltd.
eBook by : Rajmangal ePublishers (Digital Publishing Division)

Copyright © Riya Ramudamu

Table Of Contents

"

Everyone gets tired of
pretending to be happy and
ok at times. Life would be a
lot easier if we could
normalise expressing how
we actually feel.
But just keep pretending,
who cares about the
feelings anyways.

A Yearn for Rest

Days aren't the best
And nights sleepless
Life is like a challenging test
Heart screams, inside the chest
Watery eyes, wanting to rest
Craving for better, if not the best
Need a place to take some rest...

Mind full of doubts and emptiness,
Hurt and scars and anxiousness
Searching for something, called happiness
Way seems long, and journey, restless,
Need a place, to take some rest

Mind filled with pain, anger and rage,
Legs are weak, not able to chase
Willing to enter, life's new phase
It isn't easy, and hope too less
Need a clue, not sure what's best
Whether to stop or continue the race,
Just need a place, to take some rest
Small space, would be the best
A cozy place to be a guest,
Need a place to take some rest.

Good Old Days

I wish to go back
To the good old days,
Where I knew no stress

Where the days were full of happiness
And worries just too less
The life was filled with perfectness
And everything seemed the best

I wish to go back
To the good old days,
Where I knew no stress

Where the days didn't seem like a test
And there were no critics nor judgments
Life without an emptiness
Where I barely knew what's loneliness

I wish to go back
To the good old days,
Where I knew no stress

Away from the life that's so restless
Where emotions weren't so meaningless
Far from chaos and consciousness
Where people weren't so ruthless

I wish to go back
To the good old days,
Where I knew no stress

"

Just wanna go somewhere
and relax with my
solitude…
But haven't been able to
find a suitcase that fits all
my Emotions

Hypnotic Eyes

Whole world is frozen and my mind gets freeze
Those eyes; they make me go weak on my knees
That look; that just adds more drama to all of these
Why do I get hypnotized by the way he sees?

It hits so different the way his eyes glow
There aren't any feelings, but why do I get distracted
though?
I get more closer no matter how far I wanna go
The way he speaks, makes my heart beat slow

Can there be any connection? Trust me, that too I don't
know
But his name still makes me blush and glow
Why do I feel all these even I am yet to know
Am I going crazy? I hope it isn't so...

What is Love?

The more I feel, the more I wonder,
What love is?
Is it getting all the butterflies,
Or lonely late-night cries.
The instant smile, while sharing glares
Or admiring him with silent stares
The adrenaline rush when he passes by
Or the memories that always make you cry
The attention grabbing, fragrance
Or the distance that's testing your patience
The meets that motivates you to get dressed,
Or him saying "even when you're messed you look the best"
The short talks that urges you to kiss,
Or the sleepless nights where all the wonderful moments
you miss
Mind not being able to process when he's near
Or overcoming all the fear cause he'll always be there
Is it the feelings that you are trynna hide
Or feeling lonely before you go to sleep every night
Smiling like crazy thinking bout him
Or praying to see him at least in your dream
The unspoken emotion decked up in heart
Or the long and silly late night chat
The more I think, the more I wonder
What love is?

"

The entire sphere is flooded
with the shattered hearts
veiled under the hoax
Smiles.

Whimsical Weekend

Waking up late
Breakfast in bed
Messy hair,
It's weekend, I don't care

Hot bath for an hour
Singing in the shower
Reading a book,
I don't bother to cook

Ordering some brunch
Fine wine for lunch
Drinking whole day,
On my couch I lay

A romantic evening date
Goosebumps I get..
Time to get dressed
Trynna look my best

Doorbell ring
Heart starts to sing
Tight hug, long kiss
What's better than this

More wine, some fun
All the stress is gone
Soft music, dim light
Good food and wonderful night...

Such weekend would be the best
but you barely get time to rest
Weekend fun as adult is very rare,
Work during weekend, is not fair..

Just work all night and day
Fun and excitement, at a bay
Lets just hope and pray
Such weekends will definitely come one day

My heart misses you!

With every passing day
With every steps on new way
With every wonderful view
My heart misses you..

With every giggle and laugh
When survival seems hard
When I do not know what to do,
My heart misses you..

When the sky is black or blue
When my mind pictures smiling you
When my eye longs for you
My heart misses you...

When lovely couple passes by
When birds fly in the sky,
My arms yearn for you
And my heart misses you..

"

To encounter or separate is
the ongoing and undeniable
life certainty
In the end, all that matters
and remains is all the
wonderful memories and
the photograph saved in
your galleries

Beautifully Broken

I looked at the mirror today
I saw a reflection of myself staring at me
Oh! how I admired the beauty and what I could see
The perfectly done hair and outfit all set
Sweet smile pretty face no imperfections I could get

I observed a little more and something striked
I saw that she was trynna keep her sadness aside
I could see the scars that she was trynna hide
Then I saw the smile, but now I could sense her pain
The pretty eyes tired, filled with tears and vain

When I tried to observe her even deep
I was shocked and was completely deceived
All I could see was her loneliness
She didn't seem to be happy in any case
Her soul was torn and heart shattered
Seemed like no one cared about her.
Her wellbeing and happiness were never mattered

I than compared her shell with her core
I saw all the pain and emotion hurt and sore
Stong, perfect and careless woman she pretends to be
But has a fragile heart filled will sorrow one can barely see
And then I realized you could only know
Who she really is if you'll look deep within her soul

Repulsive Affection

Everytime I look into those eyes
I see the poison of disgust dripping
I feel how passionately you hate me each moment
I am addicted to your hatred

The way you speak can smoothly pierce the heart
Words sharp and blunt and emotionless
Ultimate silence like the midnight grave
I can spend an eternity communicating with you

The way you don't care about me
Raises the flames and burns my heart
No one has ever not not cared about me
I enjoy the warmth of those flames

The ignorance you behold is so intense
It has the ability to shatter the happiest of souls
It's so intriguing; I end up yearning it
It seems more familiar than my own solitude

"

There will be a time in life
when you'll feel confused,
anxious, tired, helpless,
hurt and what not
Just take a deep breath and
relax all those situations are
just making you stronger
than you ever were

Only if you could

If you could sense;
The pain behind my smile
I miss you a lot
Behind my 'I don't care'
I beg you to stay
Behind my let's end the things
It hurts like hell
Behind my 'chill I am fine'
Me praying for a companion
Behind my 'I love my Solitude'
Me craving for love and care
Behind my 'I love myself'
Only then you could realize
My loneliness and pain

Surreal Reality

The moment I saw you I was highly impressed
You would be so amazing, that I never guessed
Each moment I was questioning If that was real
I blindly trusted you tho there was a little fear
It felt so good the moment we hugged
We held hands and our fingers were interlocked
I didn't know what was going, just knew it was fun
The moment we met, it felt like all my stress was gone
I felt like I was loved, felt like you cared
When we were together, my damaged heart was repaired
It felt so surreal the moment we kissed
The happiness you gave me was something that I always
missed
The best part was, I never felt like I needed to fake
I was the real me with all my flaws and mistake
You handled me so well, I think that's rare
I might get addicted, to your love and your care
I don't like people, but I gave my heart to you
For me you are so special, which I only feel for few

"

The reason why I've built a
wall too tough and high
around me is because every
time I allow someone to
cross the boundary around
me, they teach me why it's
better to always have a
shield around.

Elusive Emotions

We get angry and anxious
We feel bitter, at times it bothers
We feel cranky we feel conscious
We get depressed and also disappointed
We get emotional and feel exhausted
We feel fear and feel frustrated
We feel guilty as well as guarded
We are hesitant we feel humiliated
We feel insecure and also irritated
We feel jealous and also get judged

We heal and we get hurt
We also love with all our heart
We feel and yes we do fall

We are humans,
Not statues or robots after all
Stop acting like an emotionless doll

Magical Reality or Just an Illusion

It just felt like you are the best
Far far far more better than the rest

I was broken and all alone in the life's race
But then you came and entered my heart's blank space

You were far more better than what I expected you to be
With you I became the happiest version of me

It all happened, I don't know how
But I am enjoying each moment with you now

You came all of a sudden out of nowhere
I would get connected so quick, I didn't thought I swear

The moment I met you I swear I was lost
It never felt like that meet was our first

All of a sudden about the world I didn't care
I shared things with you which may be I shouldn't share

It never felt like we have just met
Every moment with you I enjoyed and it was great

I was a bit crazy and so were you
I loved your company trust me that's true

And what happened next I don't think I need to say
I've started falling for you I think every possible way

"

Life Is strange:
Some Days you have
thousands of words but no
emotions to describe or
nothing to say
Other Days you have so
much to say and hearts
filled with emotions but no
words to describe them

My Love!

O my love, I don't feel right
Please come close and hug me tight
Be my light, in darkest night
And make my days shine extra bright

O my love, I feel so sad
I get thoughts, I never had
Only you, can make me glad
Need you close, real bad

O my love, I miss you dear
All I wish; that you were here
Just come close to wipe my tear
Every day, I want you near

O my love, please take my hand
Make my world a fairy land
Kiss me slow, and ease my pain
Without you the world seems vain

O my love, I feel so lost
I see the world that I can't trust,
The crowded world, is in a rush
Need you close at any cost
Just want you at any cost.

Ungettable You

I have been to various places
Trynna look for you
Every Street every corner
I didn't miss any view
Searched for you in person
Some old and some new
I just got disappointments
But I couldn't find you

Some place were crowded
At times I even felt lost
Everyone seemed heartless
I didn't know whom to trust
Routes were dark and shady
Hearts filled with lust
I was trynna find you
But my hopes disappeared in dust

The world seemed mean
I guess it's kinda fair
Investing heart and emotion
It's indeed very risky affair
Affection Attachment Care
Those shits are really rare
I was searching for you
But just got bruises and scars,
which I can hardly bear

"

How can you trust the world, when even the tapping of your own footsteps sounds like they are conspiring against you.

Yearning You

One fine day you crossed my path
All of a sudden out of nowhere
You were everything I was looking for
You showered me with tremendous love and care
I fell hard for you every moment I felt deep
But I was so unfortunate I broke your trust
Your love and heart I couldn't keep

Everything I was searching for, I found in you
Each moment I cherished it felt real and true
I would love you this much even I never knew
But I hurt both of us and all the hopes it flew
I wish we could restart again
Again like when we were new
If I want to fall in love ever again
I guess It's gonna be nobody or you
***

"

One fine morning of the blue or grey day due to differences, circumstances, situations, time or fate we won't talk to each other anymore…